CANADIAN CONTEMPORARY
REPERTOIRE SERIES

FUN SELECTIONS OF JAZZ - POP - LATIN - FOLK

LEVEL THREE

For more information about Conservatory Canada
and its programs visit our website at:
www.conservatorycanada.ca

Office of the Registrar
Conservatory Canada
45 King Street, Suite 61
London, Ontario, Canada
N6A 1B8

© 2009 Conservatory Canada
Published and Distributed by Novus Via Music Group Inc.
All Rights Reserved.

ISBN 978-1-49500-538-1

Novus Via Music Group Inc.
189 Douglas Street, Stratford, Ontario, Canada N5A 5P8
(519) 273-7520   www.NVmusicgroup.com

Preface

Canadian Contemporary Repertoire Series: Fun Selections of Jazz, Pop, Latin and Folk Music Level Three is an exciting series of piano works by Canadian composers. Level Three offers grade three and four students twenty-nine appealing pieces at varied levels within the grade requirement. Students will develop technical and musical skills with user friendly repertoire from an entrance level to grade four works.

Repertoire selections have been based on grade appropriate keys, time signatures, accompaniment figures, degree of difficulty and length. Jazz styles include preparatory rags like *Spring Break Rag*, which leads comfortably to *Double Espresso Rag* complete with stride bass, syncopated melodies and octave displacement. Boogies include works like *Dancin' the Night Away* and *A Bit o' Boogie*. *Blue Town* and *Lazy Blues* provide varied accompaniments and blues scales playing. Students will be delighted by the swing rhythm of a work like *Slam-Dunk and Dribble*. The lovely jazz ballad, *Jazzy Life*, jazz prelude *Sunset Stroll* and jazz waltzes, *William and Lisa's Waltz* and *Masquerade Ball* are just some of the jazz titles offered in this collection.

Students will be rockin' to titles like *Let There Be Rock* and *Night Walk*, while Latin dance rhythms are included in works like *Rhumba* and *Latin Smile*. Arrangements of folk songs, *The Huron Carol* and *Nova Scotia Song* provide a strong sense of Canada's musical heritage, while the jazzed up version of *Three Blind Mice* in *A Trio of Visually Impaired Rodents* is just plain fun.

The collection is compiled more or less alphabetically within genres, allowing students to move freely about the book.

Conservatory Canada wants to keep music students studying longer! We understand the benefits gained through the study of music and we believe that students will remain engaged and excited about their studies if that music is current and familiar.

This is why we developed the Contemporary Idioms curriculum. Students can now be assessed and accredited through a program that involves contemporary styles of music such as Swing, Blues, Latin and Rock.

Conservatory Canada supports Canadian composers. This book contains pieces that are either original compositions or arrangements by Canadian musicians. All the selections in this book are eligible for a Conservatory Canada Contemporary Idioms examination. The pieces have been chosen with attention to proper pedagogy, skill development and student appeal. We hope you enjoy them!

TABLE OF CONTENTS

A Bit o' Boogie

Sheila Tyrell

Fast and happily, swing the 8ths

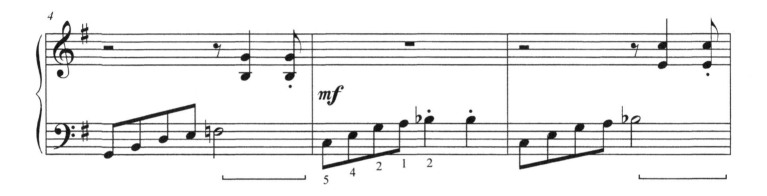

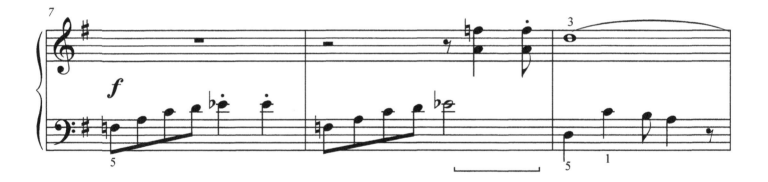

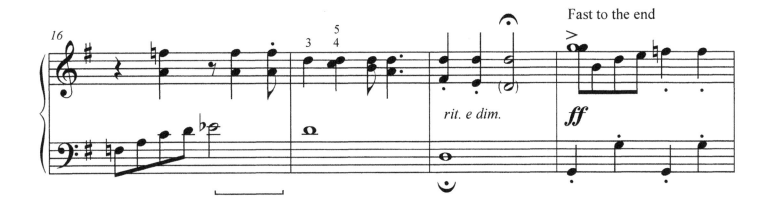

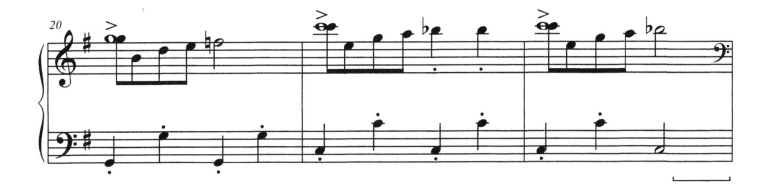

A Bit o' Boogie 2 / 2

A Trio of Visually Challenged Rodents

Traditional
arr. Brian Usher

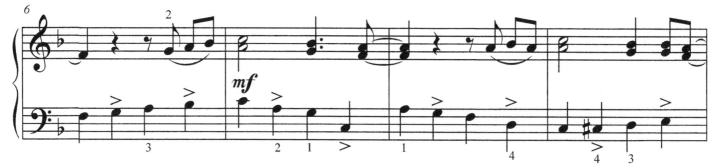

Blue Town

Andrew Harbridge

Moderato

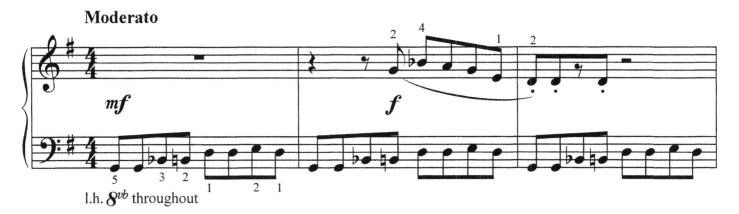

l.h. *8ᵛᵇ* throughout

Dancing Party

With a boogie beat

Fishel Pustilnik

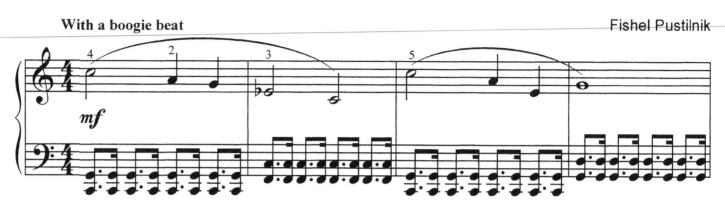

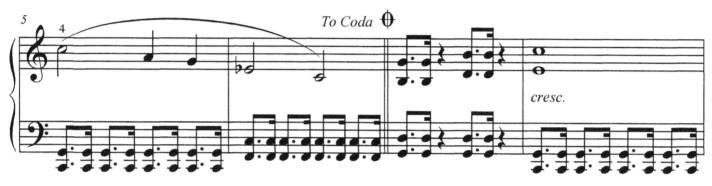

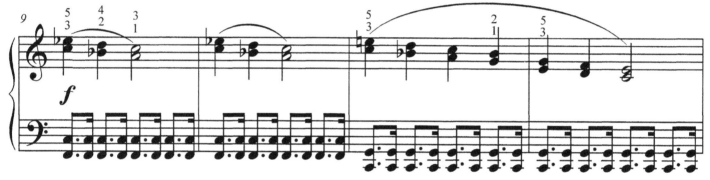

Dancin' the Night Away

Debra Wanless

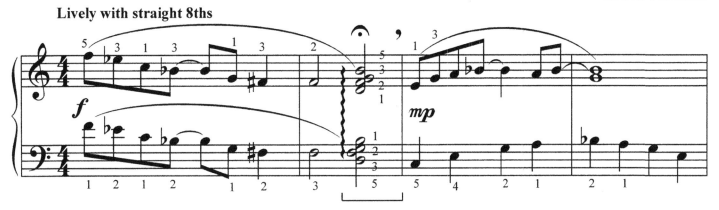

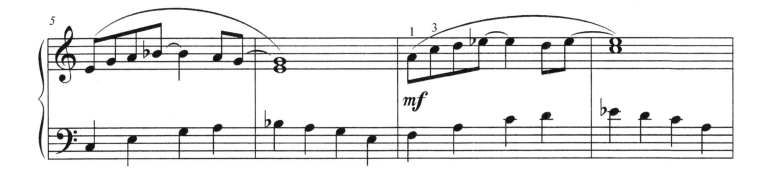

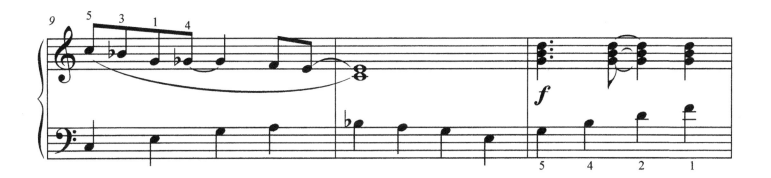

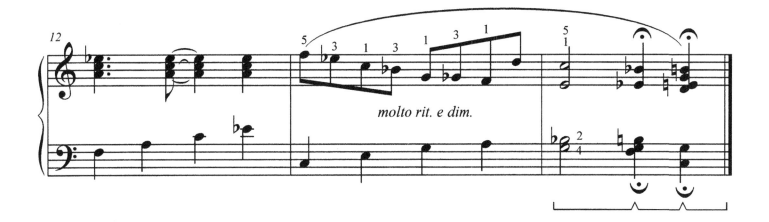

Double Espresso Rag

For Those Who Can't Sit Still

Andrew Harbridge

Fast and lively

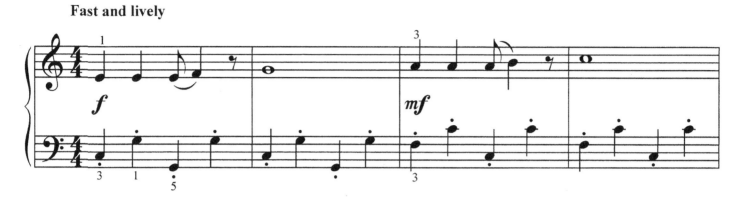

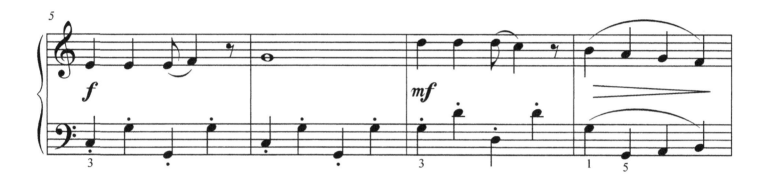

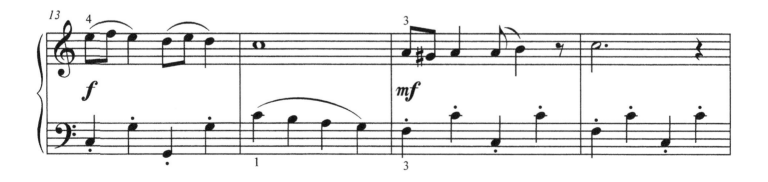

Double Espresso Rag 2 / 2

Fifths a-Plenty

Sheila Tyrrell

Fifths a-Plenty 2 / 2

Jazzy Life

Fishel Pustilnik

With a swing feeling

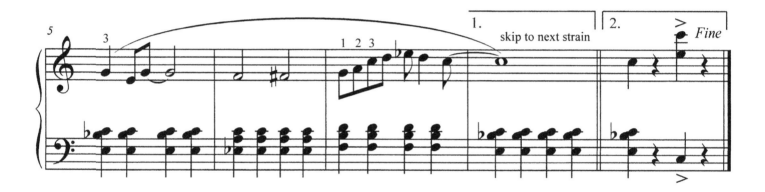

Jivin' At The Junction
for Jacob

Joan Hansen

With an easy swing

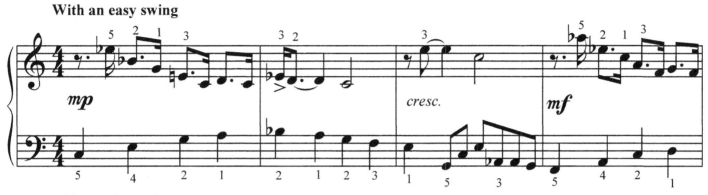

l.h. *non legato* bounce

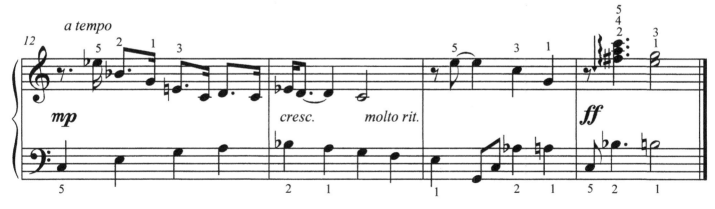

Just Hangin' Out

Joyce Pinckney

Nonchalantly strolling in the mall *

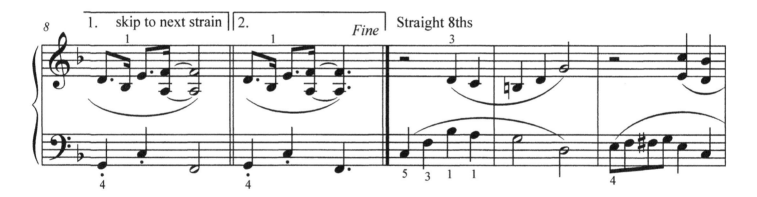

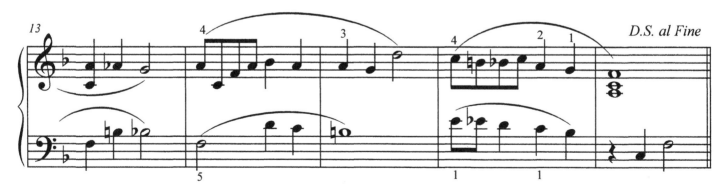

* soften the dotted rhythm so that it sounds like the first and last note of a triplet.

Latin Smile

Fishel Pustilnik

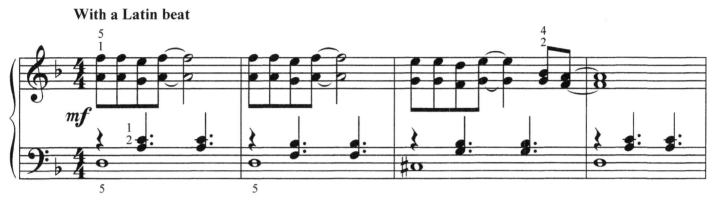

Lazy Bones

Janet Gieck

Andante, with a lazy swing

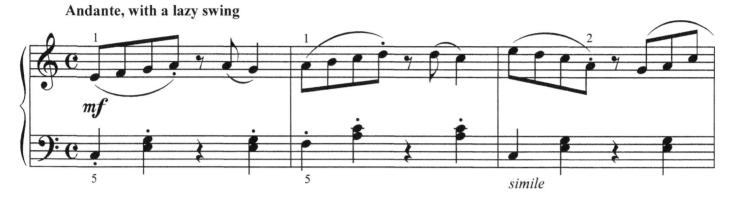

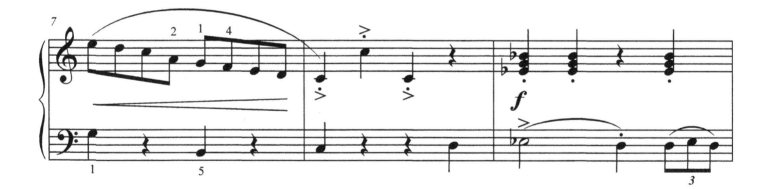

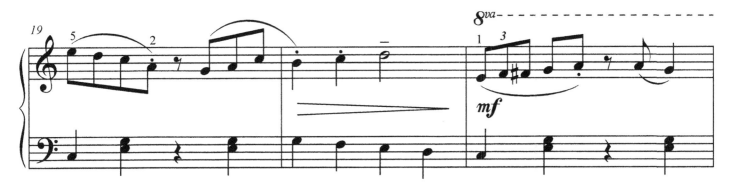

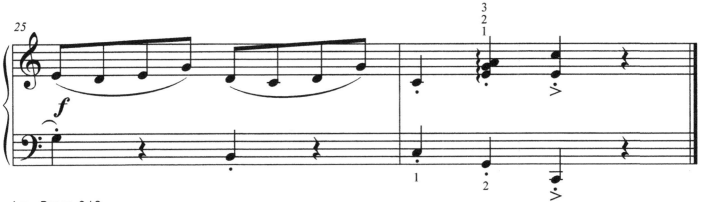

Lazy Bones 2 / 2

Let There Be Rock!

Andrew Harbridge

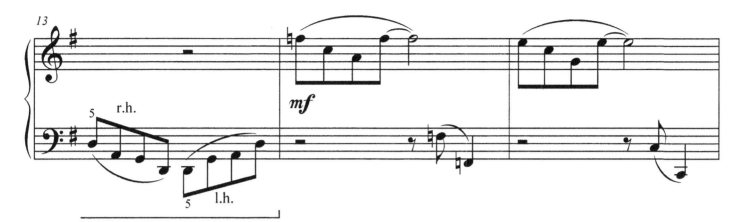

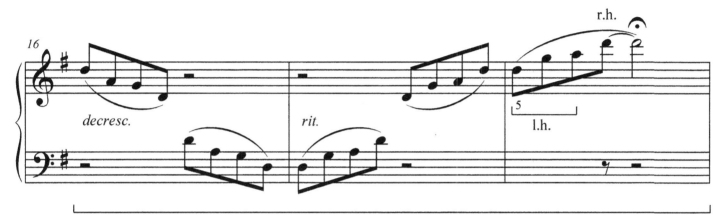

Masquerade Ball

Debra Wanless

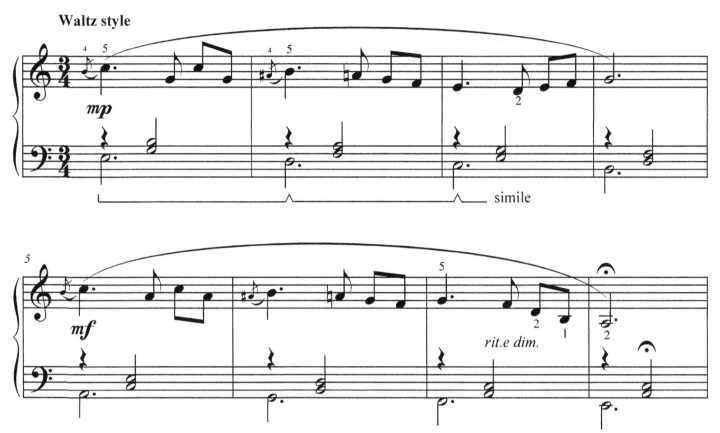

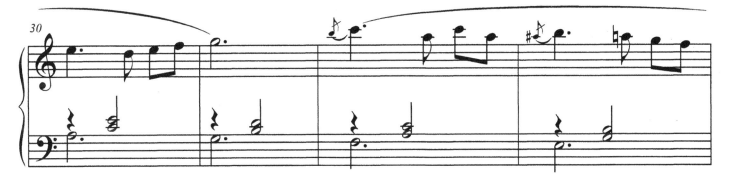

Masquerade Ball 2 / 2

Night Walk

Joseph Chung

Play the quarter notes slightly detached.

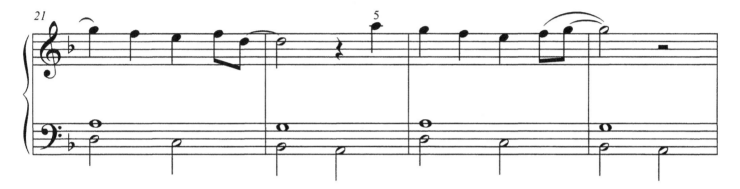

*Improvise the right hand for the repeat.

Last time *D.S. al Coda*

D Aeolian Mode

* Improvise the right hand using the D Aeolian Mode.
Repeat the passage as many times as you like.

Night Walk 2 / 2

Nova Scotia Song

Canadian Folk Song
arr. John Sandy

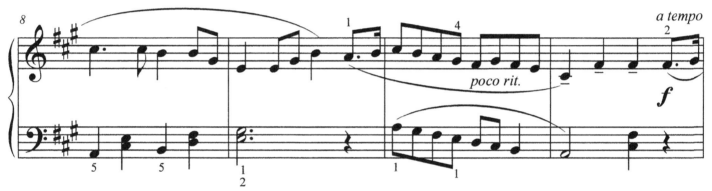

Quiet Night

Geoff Peters

Rattle on the Stovepipe

Canadian Folk Song
arr. John Sandy

Lightly swing the 8ths

Rising Fourths

Robert Benedict

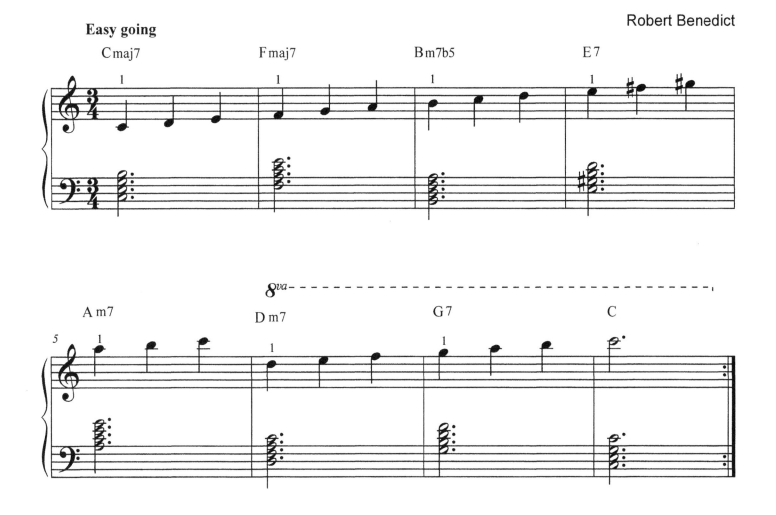

Improvisation

Repeat *Rising Fourths* as many times as you like but improvise a new melody in the right hand each time. The Chord Symbols have been written above each measure to assist you with chord names for each left hand chord and possible melodic notes.

Left Hand Chord Inversions

Play the left hand chords with the inversions below and improvise a melody above.

Rhumba

Andrew Harbridge

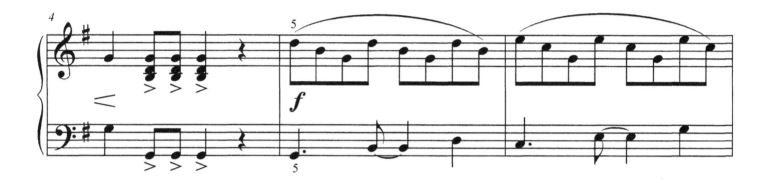

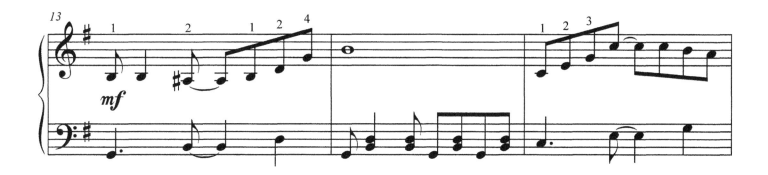

Rhumba 2 / 2

Rock, Paper, Scissors

Martha Hill Duncan

Easy going

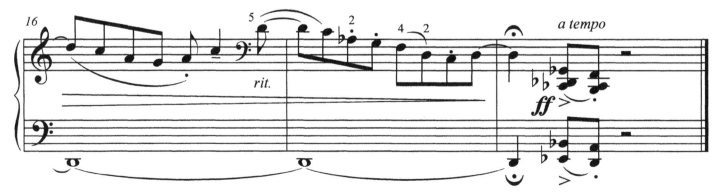

Shave Ice

Diane Berry

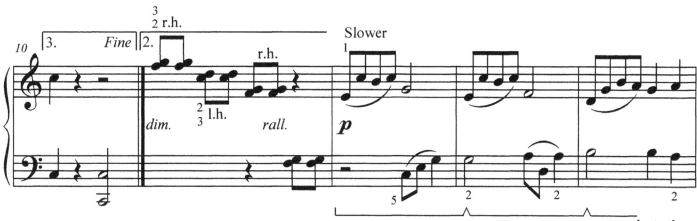

Slam-Dunk and Dribble

Joyce Pinckney

Swing the 8ths

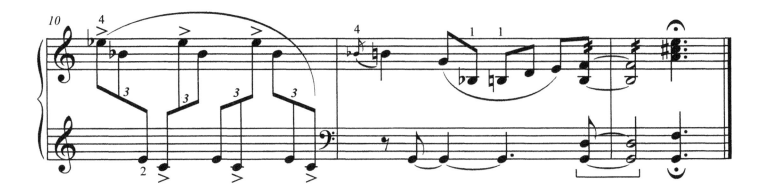

The Huron Carol

Canadian Folk Song
arr. Debra Wanless

Spring Break Rag

Sheila Tyrrell

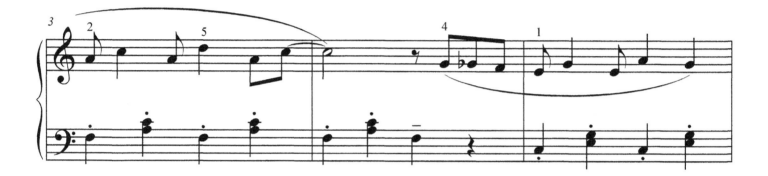

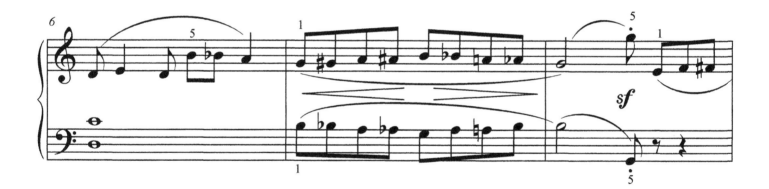

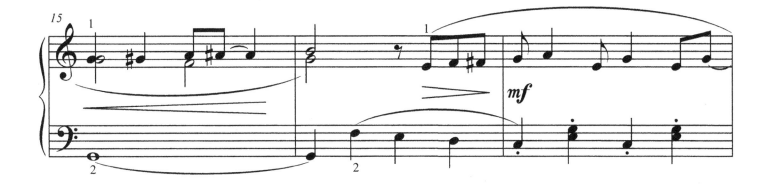

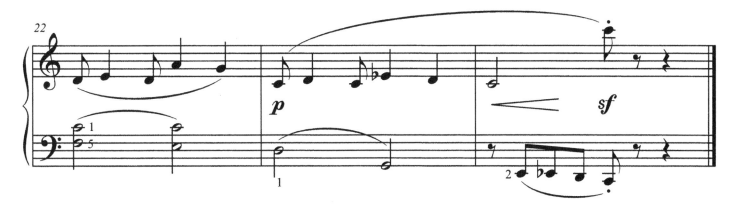

Spring Break Rag 2 / 2

Sunset Stroll

Debra Wanless

Tranquillo

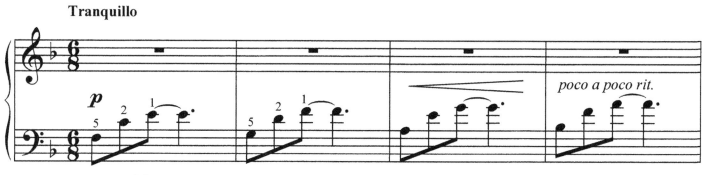

con pedale

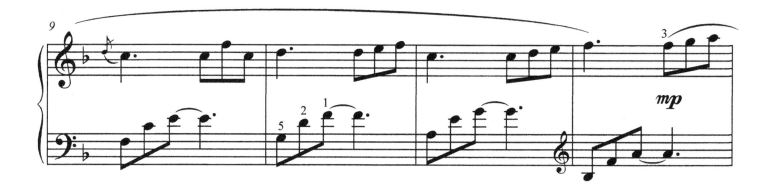

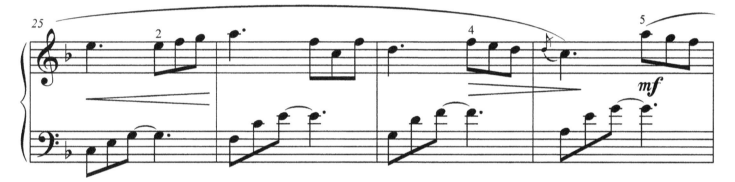

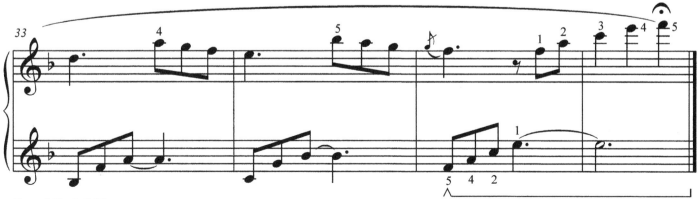

Sunset Stroll 2 / 2

The Spy Kid

Andrew Harbridge

In a kinda sneaky style

Lazy Blues

Tyler Seidenberg

Smooth and laid back (swing the 8ths)

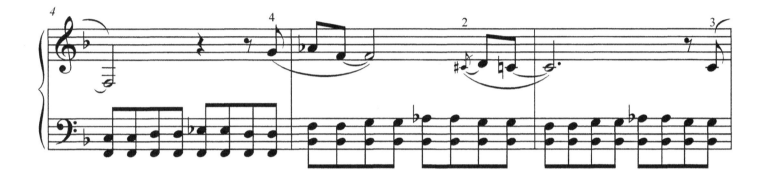

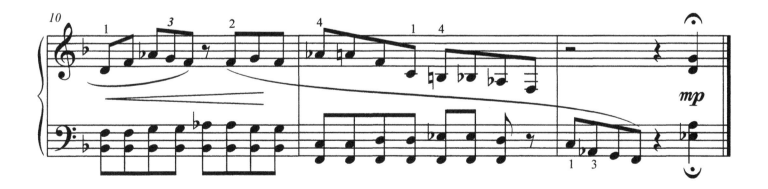

William and Lisa's Waltz

Not too fast, with straight eighths

Janet Gieck

Glossary

Ballad – is a slow jazz work characterized by a lyrical melody.

Blues – is a jazz style generally for solo voice. It was often sad and slow, usually utilizing the blues scale or notes and a twelve bar harmonic structure.

Blues Scale – is a predominantly major scale with a flattened third, fifth and seventh notes.

Boogie-Woogie – is a jazz style for the piano with a repeated left hand pattern. Boogie-woogie developed in dance halls during the 1920's and often uses the *twelve bar blues* harmonic structure.

Diatonic Seventh Chords – consist of four notes, a triad with the seventh added above the root. Diatonic seventh chords use only the notes of the scale.

Dixieland – is a type of jazz from around 1912 and is also known as New Orleans or Classic style jazz. It has elements of *ragtime* and *blues*, as well as a distinctive style of *improvisation.*

Improvisation – is a spontaneous production of musical ideas by the performer.

Modes – musical scales developed from early church music, often used and modified by classical and jazz composers. Folk music is often written in modal keys.

Ostinato – is a repeated harmonic, rhythmic or melodic pattern.

Pentatonic Scale – is a scale of five notes, often representing the intervals of the five black keys on the piano. Pentatonic scales are frequently heard in folk music and non-western music.

Ragtime – is one of the earliest forms of jazz, characterized by *syncopated* melodies, *stride bass* and traditional harmonies.

Rock – is a popular style of dance music that developed during the 1950's and is usually based on even eighth note subdivisions. Rock is the simplest derivation of Latin rhythms.

Shuffle Bass – a jazz accompaniment which moves or shuffles back and forth between the same notes.

Stride Bass – is an accompaniment pattern usually found in *ragtime*. It describes the striding motion of the player's left hand.

Swing Rhythm – is a rhythmic technique which grew out the big band era and dance music of the 1930's and 1940's. Rhythm is swung when the beat note is stretched to create a 'long-short' combination. Example: ♫ = ♩♪

Syncopation – is the alteration of the natural accent by emphasizing a normally weak beat.

Twelve-Bar Blues – in its simplest form, is a harmonic pattern organized into three four bar phrases. The harmonic pattern is as follows: I - I - I - I   IV - IV - I - I   V - IV - I - I
Colour tones, altered and seventh chords are often included within the pattern.

Walking Bass - a bass line that fills in gaps between successive harmony notes.

SIGN	TERM	DEFINITION
(accent sign)	accent	Emphasize the marked note
	accelerando / accel.	Gradually becoming faster
	allegro	Fast
	andante	Rather slow, a walking pace
(arpeggio sign)	arpeggio	Play the notes successively
,	breath mark	Break or breathe
	a tempo	Return to the original speed or tempo
(coda sign)	coda	An additional ending
	come	Like
	con / col	With
(crescendo sign)	crescendo / cresc.	Gradually become louder
	Da Capo / D.C. (al fine)	Repeat from the beginning and play to fine (the end)
	Dal Segno, D.S.	Repeat from sign (⅊)
(diminuendo sign)	diminuendo/dim./ decrescendo/decresc.	Gradually become softer
	e	And
1. : 2.	1st and 2nd ending	Play the first ending and repeat. Then skip the first ending and play the second ending instead
(fermata sign)	fermata	Pause on the note or rest
f	forte	Loud
$f\!f$	fortissimo	Very loud
(glissando sign)	glissando	Drag the finger across the keys
(grace note sign)	grace note	Play the small note as quickly as possible, immediately followed by the large note.
	marcato	Marked,accented
mf	mezzo forte	Medium loud
mp	mezzo piano	Medium soft
	moderato	Moderate tempo
	molto	Much
(non legato sign)	non legato / mezzo staccato	Not
8va ....., 15ma .....,	ottava	Play one or two octaves higher than written
(pedale sign)	pedale / ped.	Depress the damper or right hand pedal
pp	pianissimo	Very soft
p	piano	Soft
	piu mosso	More motion
	poco a poco / poco	Little by little / little
rit. / rall.	ritard. / ritardando / rallentando	Gradually becoming slower
	senza	Without
sfz	sforzando	Strongly accented
	simile	The same
	subito / sub.	Suddenly
(tremolo sign)	tremolo	Rapid alternation between notes
tr	trill	Rapid alternation between written note and note above
(triplet sign) 3	triplet	Three notes played in the value of two